THE SECRET OF OUR ULTIMATE SUCCESS

Second Edition

Ratanjit

RATANJIT S. SONDHE

discoverhelp
publishing

Discoverhelp Publishing, Inc.
33095 Bainbridge Road, Cleveland, Ohio 44139, USA
www.discoverhelp.com

A Discoverhelp, Inc. Company

Discoverhelp Publishing books may be purchased for educational
or business use. Special discounts may apply. For ordering
information, please visit www.discoverhelptools.com or contact
the publisher at business@discoverhelp.com.

Printed in the United States of America
Second Edition

ISBN-13: 978-1-59076-001-7
ISBN-10: 1-59076-001-8

Library of Congress Control Number on File.

This Book is Dedicated to
THE QUEST FOR ULTIMATE SUCCESS
DEEP WITHIN ALL OF US.

To gain the full impact of this book,
we kindly request that you read
each page in its proper sequence.

Introduction

Everyone desires to be successful in life, but we somehow have difficulty achieving it. And after awhile, the process of success becomes so complicated that the very thought of it becomes stressful. Does it have to be this way?

Typically, we measure success by the wealth one possesses or by the fame one achieves, but do possessions and fame really equate to success, and can they make you happy?

Since success means different things to different people under different circumstances, we commonly find ourselves chasing a moving target... sometimes stressing talent, other times emphasizing hard work, and still other times solely placing our faith in luck. And with so many different notions of the key to achieving success, is there any wonder that after generations of searching, that the secret still remains hidden?

This book is an instrument to help you rethink the process of success, the requirements of success, and even the meaning of true success. It is written in a simple flip-page format for maximum impact in today's highly complex and extraordinarily fast-paced world. But do not let the simplicity of this format underestimate the power of these enlightening words. Hidden within them is The Secret of Our Ultimate Success.

It is our hope that once you understand and know this secret, you will be empowered for true successes in your own life, and that you will share this wisdom with all those with whom you meet.

The key
question is
what will
make us

Successful?

It appears obvious that
to succeed, what we need is...

to find our *PASSION*.

Then...

why are millions of people
who are passionate about what
they do unable to make a living,
let alone be successful?

To really succeed, what we need is...

TALENT...

in addition to having PASSION.

Then...

why are millions of people
with passion and tremendous
talent still living below
the poverty level?

To truly succeed,
 what we need is...

DISCIPLINE...
in addition to TALENT and PASSION.

Then...

why are countless passionate, highly talented, and disciplined people stuck in dead-end jobs?

To positively succeed,
what we need is...

COMMITMENT...

in addition to
DISCIPLINE, TALENT,
and PASSION.

Then...

why are so many committed,
passionate, and talented people
with tremendous discipline,
working 16 to 18 hours a day,
seven days a week, unable
to keep their family life together,
let alone succeed?

To definitely succeed,
what we need is...

PRIORITIZED FOCUS...

in addition to
COMMITMENT, DISCIPLINE,
TALENT, and PASSION.

Then...

why do so many people with underlying passion, unique talent, extraordinary disciplines, undying commitment with prioritized focus and goals, still end up frustrated and unhappy, and consider themselves complete failures in many cases, even after accumulating worldly wealth and fame?

To absolutely succeed,
what we need is...

A MISSION IN LIFE...

in addition to
**PRIORITIZED FOCUS,
COMMITMENT, DISCIPLINE,
TALENT, and PASSION.**

Then...

why are people who are passionate, talented, disciplined, commited, focused, and guided by a well-defined mission in life, still miserable, lost, unsure, perplexed, and empty, even after having achieved their mission?

To completely succeed,
what we need is...

PASSION, TALENT, DISCIPLINE, COMMITMENT, and FOCUS, that is prioritized by a MISSION that is in full compliance with OUR UNIFYING PRINCIPLES.

Then...

why do these "Peak Achievers" and so called "Success Gurus" with endless passion, unparalled talent, discipline, commitment, and focus, which is guided by a well-developed mission that supposedly is in full compliance with their unifying principles, still search and stumble to find their way to Ultimate Happiness, Eternal Peace, and True Success?

We aren't
getting anywhere,
are we?

Maybe a story can bring us
to some fundamental realization
and understanding...

The Story of Orville Sukrat

Orville Sukrat was different. Nobody really understood him. In college he had very few close friends. He was not the smartest in his class, but always managed decent grades. He took Chemistry as his major and Fine Arts as his minor.

He tried his hands at several jobs after graduation, but was unable to keep them for any length of time. Orville always liked to paint as a hobby and spent many hours alone admiring nature and trying to capture its beauty on canvas.

Orville's family was worried about him and often wondered how he was going to make it in the real world. One of his uncles, who was very successful in business, and whom everyone referred to as "Mr. Sukrat," tried to take Orville under his wing and teach him. He convinced Orville to enroll for his Masters in Business Administration (MBA), working during the day and going to class at night.

Orville worked with his uncle for a few years and struggled through graduate school, but Mr. Sukrat could not light a fire under his nephew. Although Orville tried desperately to succeed, over time, it became more and more obvious that he was just not designed for the business world, and his time spent trying was causing Orville pain and making him depressed; in his heart, Orville knew that he was not "cut out" for business. But according to his schooling and upbringing, he also believed that he was not an artist. This often left him wondering who he was and what his real purpose was in the world. Was he really a failure?

It was clear that the expectations of the "Sukrat" name far exceeded Orville's performance, and it became more and more difficult for him to keep up. Finally, Orville decided to quit and look for a less demanding job. Orville prepared his resume and started applying for various positions in different companies.

Without a job, Orville found more time to devote to painting, which was always a tension release and a relaxing exercise. He loved going to local art shows, where he developed several good contacts with show organizers, who encouraged him to bring his paintings to display and to sell. He was not setting any sales records, but some of his paintings started to sell at the art shows. Orville was surprised that people would actually pay for what he did as a hobby; this encouraged him to devote even more time towards his paintings.

Meanwhile, Orville went on a few job interviews but received no offers. He was very discouraged and considered himself a failure.

As time passed, his artwork became his only source of income. Even though it was not an easy life, Orville became a full-time artist by default. But still Orville did not consider himself a professional artist; his style was unconventional, and he was rather unknown in his new endeavor.

Orville would often fall into a deep state of depression. The only things that could free him from this state were his canvas and paintbrush. Some of the paintings that he created, while in these far away moods were even difficult for him to comprehend, so he never took them to art shows or shared them with anyone; these paintings were his special treasures. He would often get lost in them and they became his ticket to a different world, a world where there were no feelings, no failures, no successes, no agendas, no fears, and no possessions… and yet, a world that was so complete, so serene, and so natural.

After awhile, Orville began to accept life as it was, and finally started to think of himself as an artist. He continued to meet art agents, and some liked his work and took his paintings to other shows, expanding his reach.

One of these agents visited Orville at his house and came upon his personal collection of special paintings. The agent was truly fascinated with them and convinced Orville to enter them into a national competition. He told Orville about the magnitude of this competition and the enormous prestige the winner's award carried. He described the last magnificent ceremony that he attended at the White House, where the entertainment, the food, and the celebrities all created the most elegant affair that the art agent had ever experienced. The award was even presented by the President of the United States.

Orville was beginning to get excited. He had never traveled even out of the state and was completely overwhelmed by the thought of visiting the White House and being presented an award by the President! He wondered how his uncle would view this outstanding achievement. He could hardly wait to show the world his real worth and enjoy the thrill of ultimate success.

The agent left Orville daydreaming, and it was not long before he fell into a deep sleep and began dreaming. In his dream, Orville received a letter informing him that his artwork was selected as the best painting, and that he would be the guest of honor at the White House to receive the award from the President.

Orville could barely contain his excitement. He informed all of his friends, his relatives, his neighbors, and everyone he knew. Some complimented his artistic hands, others saw his natural gift of vision, and some envied his creativity.

In his dream, Orville decided to invite his uncle to be his special guest with him at the White House. He saw himself right in the middle of the award ceremony; it was beyond his comprehension and expectation. He was introduced to famous people he had only seen on television and in magazines and everyone was congratulating him.

All of this "VIP" treatment was beginning to make Orville anxious and nervous. As the moment to receive his award approached, he started to hear strange voices and experienced a strange turmoil taking place inside his head.

Suddenly, his right hand felt as if it was under great stress. It began to shake, and from it, an angry voice suddenly emerged. It demanded that this award must only be claimed by the right hand because it had solely created the award-winning masterpiece.

The very next second, Orville felt his eyes bulging out of his head. They screamed in unison, "You arrogant right hand, come to your senses. You would be blind without our guidance. Without us, there would be no way that you could have created this masterpiece. Therefore, we must get this award!"

Without warning, screeching laughter then erupted from within Orville's head and he heard a voice say, "Without my master brain power, astute intelligence, and creativity, all of you body parts are useless devices. Therefore, without question, the award should be presented to me, the one and only brain."

By now, Orville's heart was pounding so hard that he thought it might pop out of his chest. And then he heard a loud voice say, "If I did not work nonstop to pump blood, you arrogant brain, all of you ignorant body parts would be dead. Clearly I, the heart, should be the only recipient of this award."

Then, all of a sudden, Orville began having great difficulty catching his breath, and a threatening voice from his lungs said, "If we, the lungs, do not receive this award, we are going to shut off your oxygen supply immediately! Right this minute!"

Orville woke up coughing and trembling and started to gasp in fear and anxiety. As he slowly started to breath normally again, Orville realized that he had been dreaming. Still shaking, he thought, "What a strange nightmare that was!" And although he started to feel better, Orville was still very stressed, and decided that he needed some water.

As he filled a glass with water, he could not help but notice that his hands were moving in sync with his eyes, which were guiding their every move. His heart was beating at a steady pace, and his lungs were functioning normally. Actually, Orville began to realize that all of his organs were working in perfect unison without his conscious help or involvement!

It suddenly occurred to him that each individual part and organ was serving his entire body without deviation from their specified function, and without any personal agenda or desires. The result was pure and unselfish service to the one body so that it could flourish as one being.

Then, as Orville drank his water, he looked out of his kitchen window and couldn't help but notice how the full moon illuminated the landscape with its pure silver rays, providing an absolutely breathtaking view of nature.

With all of these happenings, a strange feeling came over Orville, and he started to realize that he was a part of this nature. It was as if his body did not exist, as if he did not exist except as part of this nature. It was a very unique experience where everything was in its proper place, functioning without any effort, without any hesitation, and without any flaw. The whole universe appeared to be one, and everything was an integral part of this universal body, serving its purpose in a very specific manner.

Suddenly, it did not matter to Orville that his painting might win a national award, that he was the guest of honor at the White House, that he failed to succeed in the business world, or that he desired to be a famous artist.

As each moment progressed, Orville began to glow more and more with a feeling of total contentment. For the first time in his life, he observed and comprehended that every element in its natural condition, without exception, somehow knows its specific function in this service-based universe.

And just then, to his total amazement, it dawned on Orville that his very special paintings had only happened when all parts of his body, his soul, and the universe were in total unison, when every part, every cell, and every organ was serving the artist without any hesitation, motive or condition. Only then was he able to selflessly and gracefully serve the universe by transforming its vibes and impulses. Thus, a true expression emerged. The agent labeled it a masterpiece. And the world called it a success!

COULD IT BE...

that...

the first step
to achieving OUR
ULTIMATE
SUCCESS is...

to realize and understand
that we are each an
INSEPARABLE PART
of the...

TOTAL UNIVERSE and...

to maximize our
TRUE POTENTIAL...

we must become *ONE* with it?

Thus, to unveil
the KEY to our...

TRUE SUCCESS...

we must fully comprehend
and understand...

the basic OPERATING SOFTWARE
of this

ONE
UNIVERSE.

In other words,
we must FULLY INTEGRATE
with the omnipresent...

PSYCHOLOGY OF THE UNIVERSE

that is present within each of us
and in everything around us.

Maybe an everyday happening
can illustrate a glimpse into this
PSYCHOLOGY
OF UNIVERSE...

The Psychology of the Universe

When we plant and grow a rosebush, it requires fertile soil, the right amount of sunlight, and regular watering. It must be protected from harsh weather conditions like heat, rain, cold, insects, animals, and other destructive elements that could hinder its growth.

After this tiny plant endures tremendous strain, it grows into a full size bush so that eventually we see it bud and then finally bloom into dozens of rose flowers that offer incredible beauty and fragrance.

The rosebush has to work very hard and has to overcome tremendous hardships to, in its full glory, completely fulfill its earthly mission, successfully producing the magnificent rose flowers. And so, in the worldly sense, by creating these flowers, the rosebush succeeds. But the rosebush does not claim this success as its own. Instead, it gives the roses to all the world to enjoy.

The universe wants the rosebush to continue giving and sharing its beauty with the world, so as soon as nature allows, it buds new flowers. And often times, a seasoned gardener who truly understands the laws of nature will pluck the rose to facilitate its growth. In fact, it is when someone snips a rose that the bush has its most potential because it naturally replaces that flower with a new bud. And throughout the process, not only will there be two roses, but the beauty of the first rose can be shared with others who are far away from the original plant.

Furthermore, this rosebush does not discriminate. Its success… its mission of life… its breathtaking beauty is shared with every living creature from a criminal to the most wonderful person. Even the criminal smells the same beautiful fragrance and sees the same radiance. The rosebush's greatest success, its rose, is offered unconditionally for all to enjoy.

And by the psychology of the universe, the very moment that rosebush produces its success, it disowns it and gladly parts with it. It does not selfishly possess or hold onto its labor of love; ironically, it achieves even more success when its magnificence is shared.

Day in and day out, the rosebush simply and unconditionally remains busy producing its successes for all of the universe, without any conditions or expectations. Interestingly, the rosebush maintains its unselfish mission, even when it is raised with the intent of generating roses for commercial distribution and sale or when the growers have their own mercenary agendas.

And amazingly, although the roses are grown through the nourishment shared from the rosebush, it takes no credit for their beauty or success. Even when a gardener takes credit for the beautiful roses produced, the rosebush does not argue that it deserves the credit, refuse to bloom new flowers, or even diminish the quality of future roses. The rosebush, by universal law, is only concerned about continuing to produce the most beautiful and fragrant roses it can, making it a success.

If we look around the world in which we live, we will find that the same wisdom exhibited by the rosebush is consistent with our entire universe, without exception. We see this as the unified psychology of our universe everpresent in all living organisms, including animals and human beings, whether existing in the water, soil, or sky.

All of the universe's resources work in harmony to produce

at their full-potential when they perform according to their natural intent and design. And this is done at every level, within each element's distinct limitations and capacities, without any conditions or expectations.

What happens to us is that our human brains ineffectively utilize the limited and imperfect data received through our five senses, which creates interference with this natural harmony. Additionally, our skewed agendas cause us to hold onto our real and perceived successes, detering us from the universal process and true success.

Thus, without realizing it, we become our own biggest obstacle. We limit our total potential for success and our capability to produce the highest level of sustained success.

Therefore, based on the...

PSYCHOLOGY OF THE UNIVERSE...

our TRUE *P*URPOSE OF LIFE simply is…

to make our highest contribution...

to this UNIVERSE,
OUR BIGGER *O*NE...

by continuously
and consistently
adding...

MAXIMUM VALUE.

Therefore, in essence...

instead of being *L*OST
in our IDENTITY, our EGO,
our AGENDAS,
and our OBSESSIONS...

we must take on a...

PURE *Mission*...

through a mindset
of unconditional...

LOVING, SERVING, and GIVING...

where...

all of our
PASSION,
INTENSITY,
SINCERITY,
CREATIVITY,
and ENTHUSIASM
are immersed in...

ABSOLUTE GRATITUDE.

We are thereby empowered...

to achieve our TRUE PURPOSE of

*A*DDING

MAXIMUM

VALUE

unconditionally...

in every...

THOUGHT we conceive,

ENDEAVOR we undertake, and

ACT we perform.

And thus...

we may, JUST MAY...

discover our...

TRUE SELF...

filled with...

ABSOLUTE JOY,
ENDLESS ABUNDANCE,
and ETERNAL PEACE...

to unveil...

THE SECRET OF OUR ULTIMATE SUCCESS.

Acknowledgements:

Layout, Design, and Flow:
Jonathan A. Somich, Discoverhelp, Inc.

Design & Artwork Concepts:
H^{2}N Communications, Discoverhelp, Inc.

Photography:
Nisha Sondhe

Associate Editors:
Nicholas Stevens, Raymond C. Somich

ALSO FROM RATANJIT...

The Recipe for Stress-Free Living

In **TEA: The Recipe for Stress-Free Living**, Ratanjit brews a profound, yet simple 3-step recipe that magically helps to realign you to your naturally stress-free self.

In this life-changing novel, charming and captivating stories will lead you down a path of self-discovery to eliminate life's frustrations. Finally, the secret to living life free from stresses and frustrations is revealed! And the best part is... anyone can do it!

Available in print and audio book format!
VISIT WWW.DISCOVERHELPTOOLS.COM

discoverhelp tools
"The Power Is Within You."